2000

D1055526

Lenore Elsa
Jim Sheard

Fingerprints of Faith
Evidence of Things not Seen
by Jim Sheard, Ph.D. & Lenore Else

Published by:

 Fingerprints of Faith Press
Mankato, MN
www.fingerprintsoffaith.org

Bible References

Scripture quotations are from The Nelson Study Bible, New King James Version unless otherwise noted.

The Nelson Study Bible, New King James Version (NKJV), Earl D. Radmacher, General Editor, Thomas Nelson Publishers, Nashville, TN, 1997. Used by Permission.

Discover God Study Bible, New Living Translation (NLT), Tyndale House Publishers, Carol Stream, IL, 2007, ISBN 13: 978-0-8423-6918-3 (hc)

Scripture taken from the HOLY BIBLE, NEW INTERNATIONAL VERSION (NIV), Copyright ©1973, 1978, 1984, International Bible Society Used by permission of Zondervan Bible Publishers. Kenneth Barker, General Editor, Grand Rapids, MI, 1985, Library of Congress cc 85-50591

Cover design and interior by Purpose Design.
Editing by Heidi Sheard.
Logo for Fingerprints of Faith Press by Jake Furhman.
    www.jewelrythatmatters.com

ISBN 978-0-578-04807-9

Fingerprints
of Faith:
Evidence of
Things Not Seen

**Fingerprints
of Faith Press**

Contents

⌒ He Prepares Me: Evidence of His Power ⌒

⌒ He Uses Me: Evidence of His Love ⌒

Introduction

*I*nvestigators look for clues to determine who was present at a crime scene. Fingerprints are one of the most common types of evidence. Fingerprints leave a personal impression of who has been there and what they touched. Fingerprints are hard to dispute because they are so uniquely linked to the person. Of the 6.8 billion people on the earth, no two have exactly the same fingerprints.

> A fingerprint left behind
> identifies the one who was there.

In a similar way, God's fingerprints reveal the truth of His presence throughout history and today. Even though we cannot see God, His fingerprints are everywhere. They are proof that God was and continues to be present. This not only gives us hope, but it also brings encouragement to our faith. God's fingerprints help us know **who** He is, **what** He has done, **how** much He loves us, and **where** He can be found today. The evidence of His fingerprints strengthens our faith in God and assures us of things we cannot see.

Now faith is the substance of things hoped for,
the evidence of things not seen.
—Hebrews 11:1

Many passages of Scripture refer to God's hands or fingers creating the universe, forming the human body, loving His people, and guiding those who love Him. These passages are **fingerprints of faith**:

> *"Then the Lord delivered to me two tablets of stone written with the finger of God…" —Deuteronomy 9:10*

> *"When I consider Your heavens, the work of Your fingers…"—Psalm 8:3*

> *"…Jesus stooped down and wrote on the ground with His finger…" —John 8:6*

It is our desire that the evidence of God's presence will become more real and personal as you read about the fingerprints of God. At times the Lord gives a Bible verse, a melody, a friend, a bird's song, or an encouraging book. We pray that this book will encourage you and give you joy in the Lord. As you read, imagine the hand of God reaching out and leaving His fingerprints of love upon your life.

Human fingerprints are evidence
of a human touch;
God's fingerprints are evidence
of the presence of God Himself.

Fingerprints of Faith Prayer

By Lenore Else

*I take joy in doing Your will, my God; Your fingerprints
are written on my heart as evidence of your love.*
—Psalm 40:8, paraphrased

O Lord,

～ He Shows Me: Evidence of His Presence ～

You spoke the majesty of Your creation, Galaxies, land, and seas sprang forth.	1. Creation
You fashioned me before I was born, And placed eternity upon my heart.	2. Human Body
You gave me Your Word as a guide. It brings light to my daily life.	3. Word of God
You want me to abide in Your love. And in profound love, died in my place.	4. Love of Jesus
You said, "Come, walk, talk with Me. Tell Me the questions of your heart."	5. Prayer

You saw past all my stubborn ways, And gave me a tender, responsive heart.	6. Changes My Heart
You said to trust You with all my heart. I said "Yes Lord, make Your ways known."	7. Directs My Paths
You held my hand during the storms, Leading me to still and quiet waters.	8. Calms My Storms
You gently shaped me to be teachable. And fed me from Your nourishing vine.	9. Prunes My Branches

⌣ He Uses Me: Evidence of His Love ⌣

You taught me to serve with gladness… And to leave Your fingerprints of love.	10. Serve with Gladness

Amen.

HE SHOWS ME
Evidence of His Presence

There are five fingerprints of faith that are evidence of His presence from the beginning until now. They are ways "He Shows Me" that He is here and that He cares. They are described in the following five chapters.

*Y*ou spoke the
majesty of your
creation,

Galaxies, shores, and
seas sprang forth.

Fingerprint One

Majesty of Creation

"In the beginning God..."
—Genesis 1:1

God's unchangeable love was there before the beginning of everything. His great love preceded His creation of the heavens and the earth. The world was new and fresh and a product of God's love. Think of the awe of that first star-filled night.

"When I look at the night sky and see the work of your fingers—
the moon and the stars You set in place—
what are mere mortals that You should think about them,
human beings that You should care for them?"
—Psalm 8:3 NLT

As they walked along the beach, a couple encountered a beautiful sight. Neither could get the words out, "Did you see that?" They had witnessed a falling star against the backdrop of a beautiful night sky. God knew when and where that star would fall. Maybe it was one of the first stars He created, waiting until now to inspire thoughts and dreams. Perhaps you too have caught a glimpse of His majesty on such a night.

> As stars shine in the night,
> so His love brings light
> into our darkness.

There is an old song with the words, "Catch a falling star and put it in your pocket…save it for a rainy day." It is a daydreaming kind of thought, inspiring us to believe that a falling star could actually be caught and saved to wipe out the dreariness of a rainy day. While it is literally impossible to catch and save a falling star, it is realistic in terms of our attitude. God created this magnificent world for us to enjoy. He created it to give us a place to live and breathe. He created everything with us in mind. He put His personal touch on the grains of sand, on the seashells, on the ocean waves, and on each falling star in the night. We may not see every falling star, but we can experience the majesty of His creation and the joy of knowing that it was intended for us.

> *"Call to Me, and I will answer you, and show you*
> *great and mighty things, which you do not know."*
> *—Jeremiah 33:3*

Existence Out of Nothing

"The earth was without form and void;
and darkness was on the face of the deep...
Then God said, "Let there be light;" and there was light."
—Genesis 1:2a, 3

In the beginning, there was nothing, only a vast void. There was, however, a loving God who had a vision of what it would all look like. It is impossible for us to imagine, but God had the perfect imagination and wisdom. He spoke and the heavens and earth came into existence.

To describe how God created the heavens and earth in Genesis 1:1, the Hebrew word "bara" was used for "created." It literally means God created existence out of absolutely nothing. No one else could have created out of nothing, but God merely spoke and it happened. He created the light, heavens, earth, and seas. It was a new beginning, the first of everything.

We see the magnificence of God's hands in His creation. He has left His fingerprints in both the magnitude and in the details. They are a personal touch, evidence that "Someone" was there and left an indelible print. His fingerprints are everywhere and they are evidence God was there "in the beginning."

"The heavens proclaim the glory of God.
The skies display His craftsmanship."
—Psalm 19:1 NLT

To have any perspective of creation, you have to allow your image or vision of God to be VERY big. He is an awesome God! Just imagine; He created the flowers in your garden, the grass in your lawn, and the trees on the boulevard. He created the forests, the animals, and the food you eat. But look further. He created gravity that gives weight to all things. He created the planets, sun, moon, stars, and the parts of the universe still being discovered by scientists.

> You cannot stretch your mind far enough
> to comprehend the mind of God.
> God is greater than
> anything you can imagine.

His Majestic Hand

One night President Abraham Lincoln gazed upon the star-filled skies and said, "How could anyone say there is no God?" You too can be touched by the evidence of His creation. Begin each day with a fresh perspective of God who envisioned and created all of this. As the praise song says, "This is the day that the Lord has made. I will rejoice and be glad in it."

God spoke creation into being.
He now speaks to you through His creation.

Take time today to look on the evidence of His majestic handiwork. You will surely be impressed. What a mighty God who replaced the void with all of this! This was not a random combination of elements somehow producing an orderly universe.

You live in a world created
with forethought and love.

When God separated the darkness and created light to provide day and night, He created not only the sun, but also white light. Though white light can be quite beautiful by itself, when broken down into the component colors, more beautiful colors and color combinations are revealed. If we look a little closer, we realize God was not only an artist, but also the first and greatest physicist. Just ask those who have studied the properties of light as an artist, designer, or physics student. They will tell you that light is energy, comprised of a wide spectrum of wave-lengths. When white light is sent through a prism, the light bends at different angles, revealing a beautiful display of red, orange, yellow, green, blue, indigo, violet and all colors in between. The design and artistic combinations and patterns are endless and beautiful.

God created all the variety of plant life on earth. God designed each of these unique species with a way to utilize food, to grow into maturity, and to reproduce. While you cannot see it happening, plants convert water, air, and nutrients into a usable form. Many of these plants become food for humans or animals, both domestic and wild.

God created all the animals including mammals, birds, reptiles, and fish. There are forms of animals we never see, either because they are so small, or because they live in areas we do not visit. They are underground, in the ocean, in the skies, in the trees, and all around. What a God to have created such variety! Just to classify animals takes many volumes. Each was created with the ability to breath, digest food, grow, and reproduce.

The Creator reveals His fingerprints in the
cattle roaming the fields…
leaves rustling in the breeze…
songbirds singing a melody…
flowers blooming in a garden…
still waters reflecting the sunrise.

New Beginnings

Each day God is in the business of creating new beginnings. He allows, even encourages, His creation to change and grow. Creation is changing daily through storms, waves, seeds, conception, birth, restoration, pain, technology, cultivation, and science. There is new life every day through seeds planted, children conceived, and cells reproduced. Living forms grow and change. We grow and change as well. Our mind, body, attitudes, and beliefs change. He has created us with the capacity to learn and grow. We are in the process of becoming the unique person God had in mind when He created us. God is involved and cares about what happens to each of us.

> HOPE is *seeing* the pink of the sky at sunset,
> With expectations of a bright tomorrow.
>
> TRUST is *anticipating* the sun's appearance,
> While darkness still lingers in the night.
>
> BELIEF is *knowing* the One who caused the light,
> Continues to spread His majesty across the sky.
>
> FAITH is *recognizing* God's fingerprints on creation, hearing
> Him say, "Let there be light!"

God was there at the beginning.
He was there at your beginning.
He is there for your new beginnings.

Standing Ovation

"For ever since the world was created, people have seen the earth and sky. Through everything God made, they can clearly see His invisible qualities—His eternal power and divine nature. So they have no excuse for not knowing God."
—Romans 1:20 NLT

A standing ovation is a spontaneous reaction for an outstanding performance. The audience stands up and applauds to show their gratitude for the performance. It is a form of communication between the audience and performers that goes beyond the price of the ticket. Such a performance occurs each evening at the Sunset Grill on the Florida side of the Gulf of Mexico. It is a popular hangout during November through April as people go south to a warm, tropical climate. Nearly every evening there is a beautiful, often spectacular, sunset. People begin to gather in the early evening. They sit inside or outside and pay attention to the sun as it approaches the horizon, wondering if the sunset is going to be a "good one." The swimmers and sun bathers on the beach arrange their blankets and chairs at just the right angle to face the sun. People in condos and hotels carefully watch as the drama unfolds.

> Like the waiter in a fine restaurant
> who says "Enjoy!",
> God is saying to you,
> "Enjoy my creation!"

Quite early in the performance, the sun's rays begin to reflect across the water. The light glistens as it hits the surface. Slowly at first, then more rapidly as the drama unfolds, the sun seems to become larger and larger. The color of the ball changes ever so slowly. Depending upon the atmosphere on that particular day, the color of the sun's rays may vary from yellow to reddish orange. Then, surprisingly quickly, the last act of the performance begins when the sun "touches" the horizon. There are whispers of "There it goes!"

Everyone gathered knows exactly what is going to happen. The sun has given exactly the same performance 365 times a year since creation. And despite the fact that everyone knows what to expect, the beauty never disappoints. All eyes are fixed for the next few moments on the giant sphere settling slowly into the sea. Clouds on the horizon get into the act as they capture any remaining light from the sun. It is as if they too want to be a part of the performance.

Then, all too quickly, the sun is gone. It slips silently into the horizon as though it were swallowed by the sea. People seem to reflect on the moment. Then they join together in a standing ovation, expressing their appreciation for the performance they have witnessed. They are not applauding the sun, Mother Nature, or the entire cast of water, sun, and clouds. This is a standing ovation for the Director and Creator, God Himself.

> At the end of new day
> think of the magnificence
> of the spirit of God
> resting upon your life.

Lasting Imprints

Ask Yourself…

When did I last thank God for His creation?

Think About It…

God's throne is beyond the stars, yet He desires to dwell within your heart. Allow God to reveal Himself to you today. Feel the touch of His hands. Look for His fingerprints.

Remember…

Give God a standing ovation for His fingerprint on creation.

Respond in Prayer…

You are "Our Father in heaven…"
By Your hand You created everything.
Your majesty is written across the sky.
The fingerprints of Your work revealed.
…Amen.

Fingerprint One
Application Questions

In the beginning God created the heavens and the earth.
—Genesis 1:1

1. What are your thoughts about the *Lasting Imprints* on p. 19?

   _____

   _____

   _____

   _____

2. Pick a statement in Fingerprint One and describe how it applies to your life.

   _____

   _____

   _____

   _____

3. Why do you think President Lincoln said, "How could anyone say there is no God?"

   _____

   _____

4. What "New Beginnings" or new opportunities do you see God creating in your life?

   _____

   _____

   _____

   _____

5. On p. 15, there is a description of Hope, Trust, Belief, and Faith. Write in your own words what each word means:

Hope is _____

Trust is _____

Belief is _____

Faith is _____

6. Describe one or more scenes that have inspired you to recognize God as creator of heaven and earth.

_____

_____

7. Thoughtfully read through the account of creation in Genesis 1:1-25. Think about the scene. Imagine what it was like. Describe your impressions. What does Psalm 19:1 say about this picture?

_____

_____

_____

_____

8. What evidence do you see of God's fingerprints in your life?

_____

_____

_____

9. What idea from this lesson could you share with a friend?

_____

10. What other action(s) will you take as a result of this lesson?

_____

_____

$\mathcal{Y}$ou fashioned me
before I was born,
And placed eternity
upon my heart.

Fingerprint Two

Magnificence
of the Human Body

…In the image of God He created them;
male and female…
—Genesis 1:27

God viewed His creation and "…saw that it was good."
(Genesis 1:25) But it was not complete, so God completed His
creation in a very special way by making man and woman as
a reflection of Himself. Instead of "speaking" us into creation
as He did with heaven and earth, He "shaped" us in His own
image. In fact The Hebrew word *yatsar* is best translated as
"formed," to mold and form as a potter shapes clay. Therefore
we were formed like clay being shaped by God's own hands.

God's fingerprints are on
your body and soul.

In anticipation of this final act of creation, God said "Let Us make human beings in Our image, to be like Us." (Genesis 1:26 NLT) Being made in God's image is not about our physical characteristics, but about other qualities. We are rational, creative beings with a will and soul. We were made to communicate with and worship God, to reflect His glory.

Potter at Work

The work of a potter is deliberate with the outcome representing what the potter had in mind at the beginning. That is the skill with which God scooped up the right type of soil, added just the right amount of water, and began the molding process. God, the skilled potter, knew exactly what He was doing as He fashioned the clay. Perhaps you can picture Him kneeling over a lump of clay, carefully squeezing and pressing with just the right strength and love. His hands, fingers, and heart are at work. Imagine as each finger kneads and shapes the moist, pliable clay. By His intimate touch, His fingerprints of love are imprinted on us for eternity.

And yet, O Lord, You are our Father.
We are the clay, and You are the potter.
We all are formed by Your hand.
—Isaiah 64:8 NLT

After carefully shaping our body and all the intricate interior parts, God took the final step, giving us all we need for life. We were carefully molded to our Father's image and the "breath of life" came from God Himself. It was the beginning of an intimate relationship.

God, who created the heavens and earth,
and hung the stars in place,
formed you from the dust of the ground,
and breathed life into your lungs.

It is amazing how precisely the universe was created. Man became a living soul in an environment with air containing just the right amount of oxygen to sustain our lives. God created us to use the water He supplied. Furthermore, God gave us dominion over the plants and animals to sustain our life on planet Earth.

All of creation works
in an orchestrated harmony.
His fingerprints are everywhere.

In His Image

For we are God's masterpiece.
He has created us anew in Christ Jesus,
so we can do the good things
He planned for us long ago.
—Ephesians 2:10 NLT

God knew us before we were born. Before our parents conceived us, God already had thoughts of us and plans for us. You have the fingerprints of God upon you, and He wants to give you the gift of eternal life.

God formed you for a purpose.

God formed not only your body, but also your mind and spirit. You were not created to be a puppet or a marionette that would be manipulated and controlled. Instead, you were formed so that you would talk with God. He gave you a thought process, emotions, creative ability, and so much more.

I will praise You, for I am fearfully and wonderfully made;
Marvelous are Your works, and that my soul knows very well.
—Psalm 139:14

You were fearfully and wonderfully made with…

FEET to walk with God
…climb mountains, run marathons, play…

HANDS to serve and hold one another
…carry, wave, clap, pray…

FINGERS to caress and touch
…point, scratch, press…

TONGUE to praise God and bless
…talk, taste, lick…

LIPS to sing and worship
…speak kindness, kiss, smile…

EYES to read His Word
…see, wink, read…

EARS to hear His voice
…listen to sounds, enjoy music…

NOSE to smell fragrances
…breathe…

HEART to love God and others
…convert oxygen, feel emotions…

MIND to imagine His wonder
…evaluate, calculate, remember…

Master Designer

God created humans with three major parts—body, mind, and soul—to connect with Him. Any one of these parts is amazing, but God combined them into each human being.

Body: *The wonder of the body is in the physical design, with intricate parts and overall symmetry. It is an amazing machine.*

Mind: *The wonder of the mind is in the capacity of the brain and the range of functions it can perform. It is an amazing computer.*

Soul: *The wonder of the soul is that it was created to spend eternity with God. It is an amazing privilege.*

> Your hands formed us male and female.
> Your fingerprints are upon
> our body and soul.

Physicians and medical professionals learn a great deal in order to understand the human body. It takes years of study and practical experience to become a medical doctor. Many take several more years to study a specialization. There is so much to learn because of the very complex nature of the cognitive, circulatory, digestive, sensory, motor, reproductive, and disease-fighting systems of the human body.

Yet the Master Designer made each one of us unique. We each have our own desires, talents, and dreams. Our DNA is shared by no other. Scientists can identify us by a piece of hair, a drop of saliva, a flake of skin, a finger nail, or a fingerprint. But God does not need these methods to identify us; He knows us by name. A scientist may tell a lot about you from one piece of your hair, but God knows the number of hairs upon your head. He knew each part of you before you were even born.

Your world is His canvas.
Your mind is His workshop.
Your life is His workmanship.

Your heart is His goal.
Your faith is His desire.
Your soul is His quest.

Your Inheritance

Your inheritance includes the Father's house (heaven)
with many rooms (mansions).
—John 14:2 (paraphrased)

Your spiritual inheritance is the result of your faith in Christ. You receive the inheritance of eternal life when you believe that Jesus is the redeemer of your life, that He gave His life for your sins. When you commit your life to Christ, you have fellowship with God while you are on earth.

…You have given me an inheritance
reserved for those who fear Your name.
—Psalm 61:5b NLT

God wants you to talk with Him each day. He wants you to get to know Him better and better through His Word. He wants you to talk to Him about what matters most to you. This is a privilege, an inheritance that is guaranteed to those who have the fingerprints of faith on their heart and soul.

"Eternal Life" Warranty

There is no warranty on your physical body. It will eventually die, and in the meantime, some of the parts may not function as intended. Your mind is the same way; it has no warranty. Sometimes it works and sometimes not. Over time it may decline in ability to learn and retain information. Though your body has no warranty, your soul enjoys a lavish warranty. For those who have accepted Jesus as Lord and Savior, there is the promise of eternal life in heaven. This is a warranty that God put in writing in the Bible.

Jesus paid the premium on
your "eternal life warranty"
when He gave His life for your sins.

God waits for us to accept His gift of eternal life. Once we accept the gift of Jesus' death and resurrection, our soul will exist with God FOREVER...ETERNALLY.

"...He has planted eternity in the human heart..."
—Ecclesiastes 3:11 NLT

You were created for
an intimate relationship with God.

Lasting Imprints

Ask Yourself…

Am I living each day with the thought that I am known by God?

Think About It…

Your soul has an eternal warranty.

Remember…

You are a masterpiece formed by the hand of God.

Respond in Prayer…

You formed me to be Your masterpiece.

You breathed into me Your gift of life.

You dwell within my heart.

You have plans and a purpose for my life.

Help me to walk, talk, and fellowship with You.

…Amen

Application Questions

"And the Lord God formed man of the dust of the ground,
and breathed into his nostrils the breath of life;
and man became a living being.
—Genesis 2:7

1. What are your thoughts about the *Lasting Imprints* on p. 33?

    _____

    _____

    _____

    _____

2. Pick a statement in Fingerprint Two and describe how it applies to your life.

    _____

    _____

    _____

    _____

3. Why does Genesis 1:26 say, "Let US make…in OUR image… to be like US?" What are some implications of the use of "Us" and "Our" rather than "Me" and "My?"

    _____

    _____

    _____

    _____

4. Describe your thoughts and feelings about the creation of man and woman being like a potter shaping a piece of clay.

    _____

    _____

5. What does it mean to you to be "shaped in His image"?

    _____

    _____

6. What is your inheritance if you believe in God and Jesus as your Savior? See p. 30.

    _____

    _____

7. How are you like all other people in God's creation?

    _____

    _____

8. How are you uniquely created? What special features do you have that set you apart from others?

    _____

    _____

    _____

9. What idea from this lesson could you share with a friend?

    _____

    _____

10. What other action(s) will you take as a result of this lesson?

    _____

    _____

    _____

You gave me
Your Word as a guide.
It brings light
to my daily life.

Fingerprint Three
Light of His Word

…come and let us walk in the light of the Lord.
—Isaiah 2:5

The Bible has been called the greatest love story even written. Despite being written over a period of 1500 years, the Bible has a single theme of God's love for His people which is woven through the 66 books of the Old and New Testaments. The Old Testament reveals the story of God's relationship with the people of His creation. The New Testament provides a description of the life and ministry of Jesus.

Your word is a lamp unto my feet and a light to my path.
—Psalm 119:105

The words of the Old and New Testaments are a light on your life path. Through more than 40 authors, God revealed a timeless message for people throughout the ages. His fingerprints of love are seen in the words He inspired in these authors. God gave us the truth about Himself and our relationship to Him. These words are the direction and guidance we need to live a fulfilled life. God desires that you know Him as your Lord and have fellowship with those who share faith in Him. The message that has been set forth in God's Word is something you can rely upon to bring light to the darkest hours. It is as relevant to our modern society as it was when it was first written.

All scripture is given by inspiration of God…
—2 Timothy 3:16a

Light for the World

Light provides a way of seeing where we are going and what we are doing. It is in this sense that we use the metaphor, "light of the world." God's Word is light for our life. It shows us the path to follow. The truth revealed in the Bible tells us not only how to live life on earth, but also how we can live eternally with God in heaven.

God's Word is light to your soul.
Like a light in a dark room,
it replaces the fear of the unknown.

Like the physical light from the sun, the light of God's Word is nurturing to life. Just as plants need sunlight to grow, so also our soul needs the light of God's Word to grow. Darkness leads to sickness and death. Light produces life and growth. Growth provides opportunity for reproduction of new life and fulfillment of potential.

I have come as a light into the world,
that whoever believes in Me should not abide in darkness.
—John 12:46

God initiated the connection with humans when He created us in His own image. He formed us with the desire and capability of communicating with Him. He primarily communicates through the words of the Bible. Through His Word, God sheds spiritual light on our lives. He helps us overcome the spiritual darkness that prevails when we do not have fellowship with Him.

Just as we look to the sunrise of morning,
we should seek the light of His Word each day.

The Word of God is living and powerful when we allow it to penetrate our heart and soul. If a surgeon opens up your body, he or she can remove a foreign object, replace a diseased organ, or repair a torn muscle or broken bone. God uses His Word to perform spiritual surgery on your heart. (Hebrews 4:12)

The living and powerful Word of God

1. **Draws** our hearts to Him (Psalm 95:7-8)

2. **Convicts** us of our sin (Romans 3:23)

3. **Gives** us hope, encouragement, and peace, (John 14:27; 1 John 4:4)

4. **Teaches** us truth, knowledge, and wisdom (Matthew 6:33)

5. **Guides** our life with direction and counsel (Deuteronomy 6:5; Micah 6:8)

Light Provides Hope

Recall for a moment a time when sunlight brightened your day. It may have been while you were sitting by a window enjoying coffee, walking in the countryside, skiing down a mountain slope, eating a picnic lunch, or sitting on the porch of your home. We each have these bright spots when light warmed our face, body, or heart. It is the light of God's Word that gives hope for meaning, direction, purpose, healing, and forgiveness. It reveals the path on which we are to walk…step by step, day by day.

Without hope we are lost. We merely go through the motions; we do not truly live. Regardless of our circumstances, we need hope. We hope for a better day, but what happens when that better day doesn't come? We hope to meet someone who will love us, and whom we can love in return. But what happens when we do not meet that someone? We hope to get a promotion and a raise. But what happens when we do not get it? What happens when we lose our job or a loved one?

Read God's Word to…
know it, pray it, obey it, share it,
be comforted by it,
and receive peace from it.

In a story from the New Testament, we know that Paul and Silas sang while in prison. Also Stephen, the first New Testament martyr, said while being stoned, "Look, I see the heavens opened and the Son of Man standing in the place of honor at God's right hand!...Lord Jesus, receive my spirit...Lord, don't charge them with this sin! And with that he died. (Luke 7:55-59 NLT)

You are the light on my path,
the strength of my hand,
the peace within my soul.

These are examples of people who had hope because they had received the light (truth and knowledge) of God. They had internalized His light and hope until it became part of their lives. The Holy Spirit gave them comfort, peace, and joy regardless of their difficult and painful circumstances. They lifted their eyes and heart above their circumstances and rejoiced that mere humans and circumstances could not dim or put out the light. God can give you a hope, peace, and comfort this world can neither give nor understand.

Lord, pour Your Word into my heart.

A **lifeline** is a rope used to save a life.

It holds onto someone in danger of drowning or falling.

It connects the person with the rescue worker.

God's Word is a lifeline for saving your life.

It connects you to Him as you face the perils of life.

Without God you face certain and eternal death.

Living life is different than
reading the words in a book.

Sharing the Light

God encourages us to "bring the light of His good news" to those He puts in our path. We must be alert, available, and willing to respond even when it interferes with OUR calendar.

Let your light so shine before men, that they may see
your good works and glorify your Father in heaven.
— Matthew 5:16

God speaks to our spirit
through words of scripture
meant for us today.

Lasting Imprints

Ask Yourself…

Do I seek the light of God's Word each day?

Think About It…

God's Word is His love letter to you.

Remember…

Light is meant to be shared.

Respond in Prayer:

Your words give me hope.

They nourish my spirit.

They light my path

and bring peace to my soul.

…Amen

Fingerprint Three
Application Questions

This is the message which we have heard from Him
and declare to you, that God is light
and in Him is no darkness at all.
—1 John 1:5

1. What are your thoughts about the *Lasting Imprints* on p. 45?

2. Pick a statement in Fingerprint Three and describe how it applies to your life.

3. How does God's Word provide us with "light?" What is meant by "light" in that statement? See Psalms 119:105 for one perspective.

4. Describe in your own words how the Word of God is living and powerful.

5. Are there parts of your life for which you need some HOPE? Describe how God can give you hope in those areas.

   _____

   _____

   _____

6. How have you been able to share the "light of His Word" with others? How can you create more opportunity to share in the future?

   _____

   _____

   _____

7. Describe how you read God's Word to...
   Know it _____
   Pray it _____
   Obey it _____
   Share it _____
   Be comforted by it _____
   Receive peace from it _____

8. Why should God's Word be very important to your life?

   _____

   _____

9. What idea from this lesson could you share with a friend?

   _____

   _____

10. What other action(s) will you take as a result of this lesson?

   _____

   _____

You want me to
abide in Your love,
And in profound love
died in my place.

Love of Jesus

… so have I loved you; abide in my love.
—John 15:9

*J*esus says He loves you just as the Father has loved Him. Those words, "…so have I loved you…", penetrate the mind and soul. The Father's eternal love is the same love with which Jesus loves us. We must desire to remain, abide, and live within this love.

The idea that God truly loves each one of us is simple, yet very profound. One of the great theologians of all time was asked what he believed to be the greatest theological principle of his lifetime. With a storehouse of knowledge available to him, the man simply replied,

> "Jesus loves me, this I know,
> for the Bible tells me so."

Most likely this was a song he had learned in his childhood. You can study the Bible for a lifetime, gain wisdom from scholarly texts, and hear the messages of learned people, but the simple truth is that Jesus loves you. Let the words "Jesus Loves Me" be a fingerprint on your soul.

Profound Love

We use the word "love" to mean so many different things...I love your new coat. I love chocolate. I love you. But lasting love says *I love you; I'm here for you*. That is the love Jesus offers to you. It is love beyond anything you could possibly experience on earth.

The Bible tells us that as Jesus was walking towards Jerusalem, "He began to weep" when He saw the city (Luke 19:41). He wept for the very city whose people would be shouting "Crucify Him, crucify Him!" On another occasion, Jesus wept when He was shown the tomb of his dear friend Lazarus (John 11:35). These two incidents reveal the profound love of our Lord, Jesus.

The complete measure of such love is difficult for us to comprehend, but yet it is available for us to experience. Jesus knows your past, present, and future. He knows the pain that you have experienced. He is there for you in your sorrow. He is there for you when the world has forsaken you. His love is lasting. His love is beyond anything that you could possibly experience on earth.

Have you been touched by this love of Jesus? Have you felt His imprint on your life? Experience the love God has for you now.

> Jesus is life to my spirit,
> joy to my heart,
> and music to my soul.

All the Way

Imagine yourself at the foot of the cross. Feel the winds and watch the approaching hours of darkness. Jesus' hands flinch as the nails are pounded into His wrists. The nails secure His arms and legs to the wooden timbers shaped in the form of a cross for His gruesome death. He gasps for His last breath as He hangs on the crude wooden structure. Taken to a grave, presumably for eternity, a clean linen cloth is used to cover the blood-stained body. A large stone is rolled into place with a loud thud. Guards stand by to assure the site is not disturbed.

Later Jesus appeared to over 500 people. His followers experienced fear and great joy when they realized it was really Him. Thomas, the disciple known for his doubting ways, even touched the nail holes in Jesus' hands. He put his hand into the wound in Jesus' side. (John 20:27) The experience of Thomas is a powerful reminder that Jesus died and rose again. Jesus says to you, "Come and touch My wounds that I suffered for you."

Jesus went all the way to the grave for you. If you had been with those who returned to the grave on Sunday morning, you would have shared in their awe. His invisible fingerprints are all that remained on the shroud and the empty grave He left behind. Jesus overcame death, and He did it all for you.

He is Risen

Charles Spurgeon, the great theologian, encouraged every person to experience the same message heard by the women who came to the empty tomb that very first Easter morning. Hear the three words of the angel who greeted the women and the words Jesus spoke to Thomas. God is speaking to you through these four words:

Come

… to the place He once lay dead.

See

… the empty tomb.

Touch

… the holes in His hands, legs, and side.

Tell

… others He is risen; He is risen indeed!

Seeing is Believing

The "Jesus" film by Campus Crusade for Christ points to the presence and power of Jesus today. This film depicts the life of Christ as told in the Gospel of Luke. It has been translated into over 1,000 languages. On one occasion, Tom Axelson of the Jesus Film Project staff spoke to a large crowd in Russia following the showing of the movie. He explained that Jesus came to earth to die for their sins. By faith in Him they can have fellowship with God for eternity. Tom was overwhelmed by the murmuring in the audience and the large number of people who came forward to learn more about Christ. Tom was unaware of what had just happened. While he was speaking to the crowd, there was a clear image of Jesus, as depicted in the film, standing behind him.

When Tom returned to the hotel that night, he learned the film team at the hotel had been praying at the exact time of the appearance by Jesus. They had asked "that the people in the auditorium would SEE Jesus." Little did they realize that their prayer was being answered—literally!

The Prodigal Son

Jesus told the story of "The Prodigal Son," to a gathering of His followers (Luke 15:11-31). In that culture, the son's request for a portion of his inheritance was particularly disrespectful. It was as if he were saying to the father, "I wish you were dead." With grace and kindness, however, the father gave his son his inheritance. After receiving the money, the son left to enjoy life far from home where he squandered the money foolishly on wild living, eventually falling into poverty. Without food to eat, the son had no where to turn, but to go back home to his father. There he was greeted by his father who was waiting with open, compassionate arms.

Jesus' telling of this story illustrates the love of our Heavenly Father. He loves you eternally and unconditionally. Even though you may have turned your back on Him, He waits for your return with open arms.

> **J**= Just as I am
>
> **E**= Eternal Lord
>
> **S**= Savior
>
> **U**= Undo my sins
>
> **S**= Son of God

It Takes Two

It Takes Two is a greeting card company founded by a mother and daughter team, Georgia Rettmer and Kim Rhinehart of Minnesota. People tend to think that the name of the company refers to the two of them. But they tell people that in order for the greeting card to be a blessing, "It Takes Two," the sender and the recipient.

When we reach out to Jesus, we discover He is already reaching out to us.

This is a principle that is true with any gift. The recipient must receive the gift in the spirit with which it was given. With God it is the same principle at work. It takes two: 1) Jesus offers you the gift of eternal life. 2) It is your gift to receive. He left His fingerprints on the nails that hammered Him to the cross in order that you would not have to pay the price for your sins.

For God loved the world so much that He gave
His one and only Son, so that everyone who believes in Him
will not perish but have eternal life.
—John 3:16

Lasting Imprints

Ask Yourself…

Do I realize and accept the profoundly simple truth, "Jesus loves me"?

Think About It…

You have been purchased at a great price.

Remember…

Jesus put His fingerprints on your life by the sacrifice of His own life.

Respond in Prayer

Jesus, You love me as the Father loves You.

Your love is beyond measurement.

Forgive me for not loving as You love.

May I abide in Your love forever.

…Amen.

Fingerprint Four
Application Questions

As the Father has loved me, so have I loved you;
abide in my love.
—John 15:9

1. What are your thoughts about the *Lasting Imprints* on p. 57?

   _____

   _____

   _____

2. Pick a statement in Fingerprint Four and describe how it applies to your life.

   _____

   _____

   _____

   _____

3. Describe what the word "love" means to you. What does it mean that Jesus loves you?

   _____

   _____

   _____

4. What is meant by each of these words as used in this chapter:

   Come _____

   See _____

   Touch _____

   Tell _____

5. Describe the two-way relationship between Jesus and yourself.

6. What does John 3:16-17 mean to you? Read it two or three times and then pray about this message.

7. What does the width, length, height, and depth of God's love (found in Ephesians 3:14-18) mean to you? How would you explain it to a friend?

8. Where do you feel you personally fit into the story of the prodigal son (Luke 15:11-31)? Which character do you most identify with? Why?

9. What idea from this lesson could you share with a friend?

10. What other action(s) will you take as a result of this lesson?

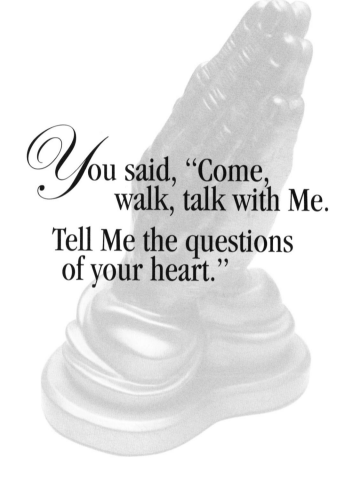

$\mathcal{Y}$ou said, "Come, walk, talk with Me.

Tell Me the questions of your heart."

Fingerprint Five

Blessings of Prayer

Pray like this…
—*Matthew 6:9a NLT*

*P*rayer is the ultimate connection with the One who created the universe. Prayer is better than a cell phone, email, Facebook or even Twitter because in prayer, you enter the very presence of God. God wants to hear your voice. In an age when we barely listen to each other, the Creator of the universe is waiting to hear from you. He not only hears our words, but knows our deepest thoughts.

God is ready to listen. He has given us the privilege of talking with Him in prayer. Seek Him with your whole heart. He waits with a gentle touch. He is ready to leave His fingerprint on your life.

Pray Like This

Imagine walking along a hillside path and coming to a grove of trees. Jesus is there and you can tell He has been talking to His Father. His face looks relaxed as He smiles to greet you. There is radiance about Him. You dare to ask, "Jesus, how should I talk to God? What words should I use?"

Jesus looks at you, gently places His hand on your shoulder, and says softly, "God is My Father; you can call Him Father also. That is why I say to you, 'Pray like this…'" He then shares with you the same prayer He gave the disciples, as seen in Matthew 6:9-13 and Luke 11:2-4.

Our Father in heaven…

> Father, it is a privilege to call You, Father. May I always live in this world as Your dear child.

Hallowed be Your name…

> May I always give glory and honor to Your name for it is holy.

Your kingdom come, Your will be done on earth as it is in heaven…

> Make Your will my will; Your ways my ways. Give me boldness in doing Your will.

Give us this day our daily bread

From Your hand comes all that is needed physically and spiritually. May I recognize all You have freely given.

And forgive us our debts, as we forgive our debtors…

Forgive me for my many wrong doings in thought and deed. May I not hold a grudge or want to get even with someone who has wronged me.

And do not lead us into temptation, but deliver us from the evil one…

Lord, as I go through this day, may I remember that You are "My Father" in heaven. May I not walk towards temptation and evil.

For Yours is the kingdom and the power and the glory forever…

All heaven and earth will bow before You, Holy One. You will return in power and glory. You are the eternal King.

Amen.

Yes, God, let it be so.

No Formula Needed

Sometimes a written or patterned prayer can seem stilted or unnatural. For example, when our prayers are a cry for help, we do not need or want a formula. We simply want to cry out to God for His intervention and help. Our prayer is merely a cry from the heart.

"...Lord save me!"
—Matthew 14:30

The simple prayer above acknowledges our complete dependence on God. We are crying out "Only You can handle this situation." We are reaching up to the King of Kings and the Lord of Lords. The gentle stream of life somehow becomes a rushing brook sweeping our feet out from under us. What a comfort to know that God hears these prayers. The peace He places in our heart is like no other peace. Only the Holy Spirit of the God of the universe dwelling within our heart, can give us the peace of "Come to Me...I will give you rest" (Matthew 11:28).

Prayer is for every moment of our lives,
not just for times of suffering or joy. Prayer is a place,
a place where you meet God in genuine conversation.
—Billy Graham

Whatever the topic, you can know that you are welcome to pray to God without a formula. Tell Him about your joys, pains, requests, insights, or confusion. Think of Him as your best friend, greatest ally, most powerful advocate, and most patient listener.

> Talking about prayer does nothing.
> Actually praying does everything.

Although no formula is necessary, prayers that take a standard format can help prepare us to enter the presence of God. These formats can help us go beyond just requesting God's help. They may take us out of our every day world and remind us to have listening ears. Some people find the ACTS model a helpful guide.

A = **Adoration.** Include prayer thoughts of worship, honor, praise, and love for our holy God. Be in awe of Him for who He is.

C = **Confession.** Admit your sins to Him and ask for forgiveness, made possible by Jesus. This builds an open relationship with Him.

T = **Thanksgiving.** Express appreciation to God for His faithfulness in all things. Gratefully tell Him "Thank You for…"

S = **Supplication.** Share your requests on behalf of yourself and others. Ask with humility and faith. Ask to know and honor His will.

Prayer Is Two-Way

Talking to God is only the first part of prayer. It also includes listening to what God has to say to us. Do you listen when you pray? Mother Theresa was a follower of Christ. She will long be remembered for her work serving the needs of the poor, sick, and dying in India. On one occasion she was interviewed by a television talk show host who asked her, "What do you do when you pray?" Her answer was simply, "I listen." The follow up question was just as pointed, "And what does God do?" She replied, "He listens!"

Listening is one of the most significant forms of communication both with people and with God. Listening leads to better communication.

Prayer exchanges your worries for God's peace.

With God you have someone who cares and listens. Unlike a busy friend or family member, He is always available to listen. He is never too busy. He sees the whole picture and knows what is best for you. He wants to hear from you and bring about His will in your life. Remember, prayer is a two-way process.

In the account of Esther in the Old Testament we are told that no one could come into the earthly king's presence unless they were invited to do so. If you went into the king's presence uninvited, death would come to you unless the king held out his royal scepter. Now, by contrast, we have a permanent invitation to enter the presence of the King of kings.

Asking God for things (petitions) is but a small part of prayer.
Confession and penitence bring us to God's threshold.
Adoration places us in His sanctuary.
There we receive the bread and wine,
the very presence, vision, and enjoyment of God.
(Adapted from C.S. Lewis)

Touched by God's Hands

Imagine your hands folded in prayer. As you close your eyes to begin to pray, you realize there is another pair of hands folded around yours. They are the hands of God. That is what happens each time you pray. He is right there with you. His Holy Spirit prays with you and the love of Jesus connects you to the Father. God's hands touch our hands and leave fingerprints on our heart when we offer our heartfelt prayers to Him.

Respond to God...

KNOW He is listening

RECOGNIZE His presence

RECEIVE answers to prayers

EXPERIENCE the character of God

BECOME more intimate with Him

HEAR His words in your heart

CARE for needs of others

The simple and profound stories of God's faithful answers to prayer encourage our faith. These fingerprints remind us that He is listening. He cares. He responds.

Be still, and know that I am God!
—Psalm 46:10a NLT

Lasting Imprints

Ask Yourself…

Do I realize He is waiting to listen to my prayers?

Think About It…

He is your protector and shield when you come to Him in prayer.

Remember…

Laying your fears at the foot of His throne is an act of faith.

Respond in Prayer

You are my Mighty Fortress.

You are the strength of my hands.

You are the lifter of my head.

You listen to the words of my heart.

…Amen.

Application Questions

...for your Father knows exactly what you need
even before you ask Him!
—Matthew 6:8-9a NLT

1. What are your thoughts about the *Lasting Imprints* on p. 69?

   _____

   _____

   _____

2. Pick a statement in Fingerprint Five and describe how it applies to your life.

   _____

   _____

   _____

   _____

3. What advice would you give a friend who asked how to enrich his or her prayer life?

   _____

   _____

4. Read through "The Lord's Prayer" slowly and thoughtfully. In fact, pray it to God, thinking about each phrase as you say it. Which phrase seems to impact you right now? Why?

   _____

   _____

   _____

5. In what ways is prayer meant to be a two-way conversation? How can you improve your prayer life?

6. Make a list of the attributes of God that come to your mind. Which one seems most significant to you at this time? Why?

7. Why did Jesus give the Lord's Prayer as an example of how to pray?

8. What do you think C.S. Lewis meant when he wrote about "the very presence, vision, and enjoyment of God?"

9. What idea from this lesson could you share with a friend?

10. What other action(s) will you take as a result of this lesson?

HE PREPARES ME
Evidence of His Power

*T*he first five fingerprints reveal evidence of the presence of God in your life. They also show an opportunity for you to have a relationship with Him. In chapters six through nine, we describe four fingerprints that are evidence of God's power to prepare you to serve Him.

You saw past
all my stubborn ways,

And gave me a
tender, responsive heart.

He Changes My Heart

I will …give them a tender, responsive heart,
…so they will obey My decrees and regulations.
—Ezekiel 11:19-20a NLT

God used Ezekiel to write that the hearts of His people would no longer be hardened like stone. In His tender mercy, God offered forgiveness and tender, responsive hearts. Those who responded with obedience were given a heart to follow God and His commandments.

Whatever controls your heart will also control your will, faith, purpose, and destiny. It is no wonder that God wants to change your heart. If your heart is focused on Him, it will change your entire life. With an appreciation for God's forgiveness and the sacrifice of Jesus, we can better realize God's fingerprints on our changed hearts. God wants to give you a heart that is softened by His tender touch and molded by His Word.

It is Your Choice

God has given us a free will which means we choose whom we will follow and whom we will obey. God may put things and events in our path, but ultimately He allows us to choose.

The choice we have to make is whether or not we will open up our heart to God. This is a decision that we alone must make. Our parents, spouse, or children may love the Lord, but we cannot coast to heaven on their choice. The choice is ours alone. The consequences are also ours alone.

> God wants to change your heart,
> but you have to want to change.

What does it mean to want to change? It means being open to God and to His Word. It means more than just passive acceptance, but actively seeking after Him. Ask the Holy Spirit to give you truth, help you to understand, and open your eyes to His plans for you. Ask Him to put people in your life who will help you on the journey of faith and faithfulness.

> If you open the door of your heart,
> He will enter and give you hope.
> An open heart is waiting
> to be filled with new life.

The Heart of the Matter

"The heart of the matter" is the core of the topic. This same connotation is used in the Bible. Matters of the heart are extremely important in God's eyes. God did not intend to give His people a new physical heart. Instead, God is concerned about your spiritual heart. It is the core of passion and enthusiasm in a believer. It worships God with a full awareness of His great love. Jesus wants to be at the center of your heart where He can give you spiritual oxygen and food for your soul.

God wants you to have a clean, pure, and humble heart. We are to be faithful with our whole heart. The Bible uses the word "heart" to refer to the direction we are to go in life.

"…incline your heart to the Lord God…"
—Joshua 24:23

God grants forgiveness and offers a new life and a new heart to those individuals who accept the grace of Jesus. This gift is available to all of the people of God's creation, not just the chosen people of Israel.

Jesus gave His life for you.
He is waiting for you to give Him your heart.

Open Heart Surgery

We can better understand the hardening and renewal of the spiritual heart by looking at our physical heart. In medical terms, the heart refers to that part of the body that pumps the blood throughout the body. From its location in the chest cavity, this critical part of the body is the pumping station that is responsible for distribution of life-giving oxygen and food for cells. Those cells located throughout the body rely on this daily supply and in turn use the circulating blood to return carbon dioxide to the lungs for exhaling.

> *"...Today, if you will hear His voice,*
> *Do not harden your hearts..."*
> —Hebrews 3:7-8

We know that one condition of the heart that stops its proper functioning is the hardening of the coronary arteries. These hardened arteries block the flow of blood and therefore reduce the exchange of life-giving blood for the cells. This is spiritually analogous to what happens when we seek our own desires rather than exchanging them for God's desires.

A man recalling his open heart surgery stated:

> *"As I look back to the years before my surgery I can see I wasn't really paying attention to or taking seriously how I took care of myself. I can see that happening to*

me spiritually as well. If I don't pay close attention to my walk with God, my time in His Word and prayer, and have regular check-ups with other men to keep me accountable, then my spiritual arteries get clogged up over time. Open heart surgery made me take a serious look at how I was doing spiritually, not just physically. I not only had a physical bypass, but a spiritual one as well."

God desires to give each of us a "change of heart." A changed heart involves the core of our being. God desires our spiritual heart to become soft and remain responsive to His Word. He wants us to function as a part of the body of Christ. He wants us to know the Word, grow in Him, and be ready for His return.

Like the people of the Old Testament, we can become cold and stony of heart when we fail to study and follow His Word. We also become cold of heart when our lives are absent of thoughts of God, fellowship, and accountability with other believers. That is when spiritual open heart surgery is needed.

> *"…For the Lord does not see as man sees;*
> *for man looks at the outward appearance,*
> *but the Lord looks at the heart."*
> —*1 Samuel 16:7*

People with a new heart will "obey my decrees and regulations" (Ezekiel 11:20a). They will be men and women after God's own heart. They will want to know His Word and seek after Him.

The evidence will reflect a heart that is influenced by Jesus Christ. The changes will include your 1) prayer life, 2) relationships, and 3) use of time and money. Some evidence will be private and some will be visible to others. The real point is that you desire to be changed by the love of Christ.

> *"Wherever your treasure is,*
> *there the desires of your heart will also be."*
> *—Matthew 6:21 NLT*

Are you being renewed by the transforming power of God at work in your life? Change will come when you offer Him a receptive and tender heart.

Changing your heart is a lifelong process.

Lasting Imprints

Ask Yourself…

Do I give my heart to God each morning?

Think About It…

When your heart is changed, your relationships change.

Remember…

When you love with all your heart, there are no spaces waiting to be filled.

Prayer of Response

The door of my heart is open.

Enter in and be my King.

Fill me with Your Spirit.

Make me responsive to Your will.

…Amen.

Fingerprint Six
Application Questions

*"I will take away their stony, stubborn heart and
give them a tender, responsive heart,
so they will obey My decrees and regulations."*
—Ezekiel 11:19-20a NLT

1. What are your thoughts about the *Lasting Imprints* on p. 81?

2. Pick a statement in Fingerprint Six and describe how it applies
    to your life.

3. What is the meaning of 1 Samuel 16:7?

4. Contrast the differences between a "hardened heart" and a
    "tender and responsive heart."

    On a ten point scale (0=totally hardened, 10=totally tender)
    what number would describe your heart today? Why?

5. What does it mean to have an open or a closed heart? How can you open your own heart to the Lord?

    _____

    _____

6. How would you describe spiritual open heart surgery? Have you experienced it?

    _____

    _____

7. What does Matthew 6:21 mean to you?

    _____

    _____

    Where are the treasures of your life? Are there any God would want you to give up or add to your list?

    _____

    _____

8. Giving your heart to Jesus is a one-time, daily, <u>and</u> continuous process. Why are all three statements correct?

    _____

    _____

9. What idea from this lesson could you share with a friend?

    _____

    _____

10. What other action(s) will you take as a result of this lesson?

    _____

    _____

You said to trust You
 with all my heart.

I said, "Yes, Lord,
make Your ways known."

He Directs My Paths

"…He shall direct your paths."
—Proverbs 3:5-6

Major choices in life include what we will do for a career, where we will live, whom we will marry, and what we will do with our money. Sometimes we have the opportunity to select from alternatives and other times there are no alternatives. The designated path is thrust upon us without any input on our part.

We make our choices based upon our experience, knowledge, and help from friends and advisors. But for the person who seeks after God, there is a better source of guidance. God directs the paths of those who trust in Him and acknowledge Him as their Lord. They give Him the reins when it comes to choosing important pathways and decisions.

God is the best source of direction for your life. He knows everything about your past, your present, and your future. He knows all the options you will face throughout your life. When you put your life in His hands, you can know that He will provide direction. When you follow God's lead, you are changed in ways that are both pleasing to Him and also best for you. In this process, you become more like Jesus.

Give God your priorities.

In God We Trust

"In God We Trust" is printed on our money, but we seldom read or think about what it means. Psalm 25 begins, "To You, O Lord, I lift up my soul. O my God, I trust in you." If we truly lift up our souls before the Lord, we are presenting ourselves as a living sacrifice. We are saying "Here I am…I am ready to follow Your will. I am holding nothing back. I am giving You my past, my present, and my future."

Psalm 25:4-5 reveals three key ways we can seek to demonstrate our trust in God. Ask God: "Show me Your ways, teach me Your paths, and lead me in Your truth."

He Shows Me His Ways

Psalms 25:4a reads, "Show me Your ways, O Lord." David asks God to reveal His intentions and plans. He wants to know God's "ways" as it relates to his own life. David knows that God's ways are just, righteous, (Deuteronomy 32:4) and everlasting. (Psalm 139:24)

David is seeking the will of God and wants to be a participant in God's plans. To participate with God, we must allow Him to take our hand in His. It's as though a landscape artist lets us watch as he paints. He then lets us feel his hand as he paints the scenery. Finally, he hands us the paint brush and says "Let's paint together, while my hand remains upon yours." God is like that artist showing us His ways.

A sous-chef de cuisine is an assistant to an executive chef. Working under the direction of the top chef, the sous-chef watches as the executive shows him or her how to prepare each dish. He or she then does exactly what is expected of them. The sous-chef imitates the way the dish is stirred, remembers which spices are used, sets the proper oven temperature, and much more. Only in this way is the sous-chef able to repeat each dish exactly as it was demonstrated by the mentor.

"…Show me your ways…" indicates that David seeks after God with all his heart. David wants to "know God's ways." Here, "ways" encompasses His character, purpose, style, approach, and way of relating with people. It is a lifelong process of growing and knowing God. David was learning, as we should learn, that God never acts out of character, nor does He ever change.

> *"He who has begun a good work in you will complete it...*
> *until the day of Christ."*
> —*Philippians 1:6 NLT*

He Teaches Me His Paths

The Psalmist continues to ask God to allow him to participate in achieving His will. He asks God to "...teach me Your paths." *Paths* are more specific than *ways*. Paths are routes, directions, and courses of action throughout life.

The "paths" of our lives involve choices regarding 1) the **direction** we will travel and 2) the **method** to get to the destination. If you trust in God, you want to learn the direction and plans He has in mind for you. You know that He wants the very best for you and will show you the path that is best. He may not put up big and bright road signs, but He will be there to help guide you.

For example, hikers study the path they will take and the proper activities for safe hiking. With advice from experienced hikers and a map they can count on, they know they will reach their final destination. They read the trail and do not stray from their charted course. Likewise, we should follow the path God teaches us.

He Leads Me in His Truth

Psalms 25 says, "Lead me in Your truth, and teach me..." God has presented His truth to us in the Bible. If we know God's truth, it will help us to know His ways and His paths as they apply to our lives. Knowing God's truth is the most important information you could possibly have, especially if your goal is to trust God in all matters of your life.

A GPS, global position system, is a remarkable technology available to us today. The small device with a screen and navigation system is tied to a network of satellites, keeping the unit updated on your location at all times. The programming allows you to follow directions as you go from one point to another. The device shows and announces all the right streets and turns until the final destination is reached. The user assumes that the information is accurate, but sometimes either the roads have been changed or the user makes an error in inputting the address data. Likewise, our spiritual GPS system must always be set on the right destination in order to achieve the right goals. That means that we, like David, must set our course on God's truth.

> God's Positioning System (GPS)
> guides you to truth.

Jesus, A Model to Follow

We don't know what Jesus looked like nor do we know what clothes He wore. While there are many artists' renditions of Him, they are all speculations. Regardless of His actual appearance, the way Jesus lived, thought, spoke, and related to people, are fingerprints of God.

"Do you not know that I must be about my Father's business?"
—Luke 2:49

Are you leaning on your own understanding or trusting the Lord with all your heart?

How did Jesus go about His Father's business? How does it serve as a model for our own life?

1. **Jesus put His heavenly Father first in His life.**
   Jesus spoke and did what His Father wanted Him to do. He walked according to His Father's shadow.

2. **Jesus knew the Word of God and quoted it often.**
   Jesus quoted scripture when giving guidance on how to live life. He even quoted it when He was tempted. For our own guidance and protection we also need to know Scripture.

3. **Jesus prayed daily.**
   Jesus prayed to His Father daily. He spent much time in prayer and even prayed all through the night before

choosing His twelve disciples. (Luke 6:12) The decisions that affect our lives and the lives of others would be much different if we also spent the night in prayer.

4. **Jesus loved, touched, healed, and forgave.**

As we walk in Jesus' shadow, we would follow His model of loving those who appear unlovable. We would place a loving touch upon those who are hurting. We would forgive because He forgave us.

5. **Jesus wept.**

Jesus wept before He raised Lazarus from the dead (John 11:35) and He wept over the city of Jerusalem. (Luke 19:41) Walking in Jesus' shadow will bring times of shedding tears for us as well.

6. **Jesus rested.**

When you are carefully walking in the shadow of Christ, there will be times when His shadow stops moving. Sometimes this means that the best action for you is to do nothing but wait. It may also mean that God wants you to rest for one reason or another. He may want to teach or refuel you for the next move. John 7:37-38 tells us if we are thirsty, we can come to Him and be refreshed. His refreshing pause causes "rivers of living water" to flow within us.

Have you ever played the game of walking in someone's shadow? With the sun directly in front of them, their long shadow trails behind. Your goal is to keep walking on their shadow one step at a time without lagging behind or going ahead of their movement. You move only when the shadow moves. It's fun as you try to walk on the moving shadow. Regardless of how well you do, you cannot control the shadow. In following Jesus, we need to be alert as He directs when and where to place our steps. In the game, just as in following Christ, we are not to get ahead or lag behind. It is a nice reminder that Jesus lived His life in the light so we could walk in His shadow.

Lord, help me to walk in Your shadow
and be about my Heavenly Father's business.

"Remember, each moment is a new beginning.
Your future is not defined by your past.
Your thoughts can change, and consequently,
Your future life can become totally different."
—Tommy Newberry

Lasting Imprints

Ask Yourself...

Do I sense Jesus' fingerprints directing my path?

Think About It...

Becoming like Jesus requires following His guidance, listening to His teaching, and watching for His fingerprints

Remember...

When you trust in Him, the light for your path comes from God's Word.

Respond in Prayer

Show me Lord... I'll watch.

Teach me Lord... I'll listen.

Guide me Lord... I'll follow.

You are the Way, Truth, and Life.

...Amen.

He Directs My Paths

Trust in the Lord with all your heart,
And lean not on your own understanding;
In all your ways acknowledge Him,
And He shall direct your paths."
—Proverbs 3:5-6

1. What are your thoughts about the *Lasting Imprints* on p. 93?

   _____

   _____

2. Pick a statement in Fingerprint Seven and describe how it applies to your life.

   _____

   _____

   _____

3. How is the term "paths" used in this chapter and in Scripture?

   _____

   _____

4. What are the various kinds of "paths" that are important in your life right now? (Consider career, family, friends, spiritual, etc.) To what extent has each of these been directed by God, by you, or by others?

   _____

   _____

   _____

5. Read Psalm 25 and meditate on it in your prayers. Describe any thoughts or ideas God gives you about your ways, paths, and understanding of truth.

_____

_____

_____

6. There are six ways Jesus modeled His life after God presented in this chapter. Pick one of the ways and describe how it applies to your life.

_____

_____

_____

7. Read the Tommy Newberry quote from _The 4:8 Principle: The Secret to a Joy-Filled Life_ on p. 92. What does it mean to you?

_____

_____

8. "Shows Me," "Teaches Me," and "Leads Me" are used extensively in this chapter. In what ways are these three similar to one another? In what ways are they different from one another?

_____

_____

_____

9. What idea from this lesson could you share with a friend?

_____

10. What other action(s) will you take as a result of this lesson?

_____

_____

You held my hand
        during the storms,

Leading me to still
and quiet waters.

He Calms My Storms

"...the wind ceased and there was a great calm."
—Mark 4:39

Jesus was standing on a boat near the edge of the Sea of Galilee telling parables about the Kingdom of God. When evening came Jesus asked the disciples to take Him to the other side of the lake. It must have been an exhausting day because Jesus fell asleep as they crossed the lake. A fierce storm arose without warning. The frightened disciples shouted to Jesus, "Teacher, do you not care that we are perishing?" Jesus awoke and rebuked the wind and told the sea, "Peace, be still!" Immediately, the wind ceased and the lake was calm.

Jesus is already in the boat with you.
He has not left you alone to face the storm.

We may experience a variety of storms, events, and circumstances that come without notice. We may be frightened, alarmed, and tossed around on a "stormy sea." When we cry out, Jesus is with us in the midst of our storms. He is there to calm the sea.

"Call upon Me in the day of trouble;
I will deliver you, and you shall glorify Me."
—Psalm 50:15

Storms We Face

Our hardships and challenges are the storms we face of a different type. They too toss us around. Feelings of helplessness or incompetence grow as we lose control and struggle to survive. Often these stormy situations bring fear. They even challenge our faith as they did for the disciples.

Some of the storms include challenges in relationships, finances, and workplaces. Other storms come from forces within our body—sickness, self-doubt, inner turmoil, and stress. These storms make us feel as if we are attempting to stay upright against gale-force winds.

> During the storms of your life,
> His voice is saying, "Peace, be still!"

Many people find it difficult to believe that a loving and powerful God would allow terrible "storms" to create havoc in our lives. They say there must not be a God because he would not allow all the catastrophes that occur in the world. Some people have personal tragedy in their own life which they believe a loving and powerful God would not have allowed. For example, a lady told Jim she had suffered the loss of a daughter, granddaughter, and other family members. Despite praying over and over to God, He still allowed those terrible things to happen. She honestly questioned, "Why should I trust such a God?"

The answer is given by Peter when he said to Jesus, "Lord, to whom do we turn? You have the words of eternal life." We must trust that even when we feel alone in the violence of the storm, God is there. God is in control.

> The sun reflects
> even in the puddles of life.

God will atone for every single one of your tears. First,
the reason behind your suffering will be made plain as
God reveals something so glorious in His purpose that
it will completely suffice for all your hurt. Next, as God
dries your tears, it will showcase the intimate, sweet
affection of God toward you personally—much more so
than if you never cried.

—Joni Erickson Tada

God does not always give us the peace we desire. Some storms cannot be avoided or understood. We simply have to recognize that His ways are higher than our ways. We have to trust that He is in charge. He will work out the details. We are to pray, to listen, and to trust Him for our well-being. Storms may help teach us important lessons to strengthen our faith and prepare us for future circumstances. Remember, the storm arose despite the fact that the disciples were following Jesus' instructions to go across the Sea of Galilee.

Though I walk in the midst of trouble, You will revive me.
—Psalm 138:7

Even though we follow the Almighty God, we are not promised an easy life. Paul writes in Acts 14:22 that the follower of Christ will endure hardships. The psalmist points out that we will experience dark valleys, enemies, and evil forces. In 1 Peter 4:12 the message is much the same. Peter says that you should not be surprised when you encounter trials, enemies, or even death itself. Those who seek the narrow path of following the Lord in faith, and engage in the spiritual battle against evil, will have similar challenges to those faced in the Old and New Testament.

> ### Storms bring maturity to
> ### our relationship with God.

God can use difficult situations as a way of accomplishing His purpose in our life. King David turned to God in times of trouble. He wrote, "The Lord will perfect that which concerns me." (Psalm 138:8)

> ### God gives us comfort
> ### when we are receptive to Him.

Be advised, if you're going to be a…

SAILOR…you're going to have ROUGH SEA.S

CHEF…you're going to have HEAT IN THE KITCHEN.

PILOT…you're going to have TURBULENCE.

CHAMPION…you're going to have PAIN.

FARMER…you're going to have WEEDS.

FOOTBALL PLAYER…you're going to have HARD HITS.

CHRISTIAN…you're going to have SUFFERING.

Find Calm Waters

The 23rd Psalm explains the peace and contentment God wants you to experience. Some of the key words and phrases are in bold letters below to help guide your reading of this passage.

Psalm 23 NLT

The Lord is **my shepherd**;

I have all that I need.

He **lets me rest** in green meadows;

He **leads me** beside peaceful streams.

He **renews** my strength.

He **guides me** along right paths, bringing honor to His name.

Even when I walk through the darkest valley,

I will **not be afraid,** for You are close beside me.

Your rod and Your staff **protect and comfort me.**

You prepare a **feast** for me in the presence of my enemies.

You **honor me** by anointing my head with oil.

My cup overflows with **blessings.**

Surely Your **goodness and unfailing** love

will pursue me all the days of my life,

and I will **live in the house of the Lord** forever.

"Peace I leave with you, My peace I give to you;
not as the world gives do I give to you.
Let not your heart be troubled, neither let it be afraid."
—John 14:27

The shepherd kept his sheep away from fear and darkness. He took the sheep to the pastures of the high ground where they could graze in comfort. The shepherd's rod was a means of defending the sheep against enemies. The staff, on the other hand, was used to keep them from wandering away. It could also draw them back from danger. These words from God through the psalmist, provide assurance of His love and care.

> *"...I have been led to an inner place where I had not been before. It is a place within me where God has chosen to dwell. It is a place where I am held safe in the embrace of an all loving Father who calls me by my name and says, 'You are my beloved..., on you rests my favor.' It is a place where I can taste the joy and peace that are not of this world."*
>
> —Henri Nouwen

Rainbow of Love

God conveyed His heart of love through the symbolism of the rainbow. After Noah's family and the animals on the ark survived the flood, God refracted the light through the vapor of the sky to create the first rainbow. It was God's symbol of love and His promise to not send another flood to cover the entire earth.

> Even in the midst of dark clouds,
> there is a rainbow overhead.

Lenore was enjoying a boat ride with her family on a beautiful summer afternoon. She relates,

> *For some reason, I was allowing sad and discouraging thoughts to fill my mind and disturb my enjoyment of the day. As I dwelled upon these thoughts, tears filled my eyes and slowly dripped down until they gathered in the lower rim of my sunglasses. The sun's reflective rays through the sunglasses and tears caused my eyes to behold a beautiful, private rainbow. God had taken my tears and turned them into an immediate reminder of His presence. He was there to calm the storms of my heart. He is always there for me.*

> God removes our storms
> and gives us His rainbow of love.

Recall the storms He has calmed in your life. Have you stopped to thank God for the hope He has given following a storm? He displays magnificent reminders of His awesome power, as well as His tender love and care. Thank Him. Ask Him to help you deal with the storms you are facing.

> As the sunrise changes the dark clouds
> into pink and blue;
> You come to give me hope
> in the darkest of night.

May God go **before** you to give light to your path.

May He be **behind** you to encourage you.

May He be **beside** you to befriend you.

May He be **above** you to watch over you.

May God Almighty be **within** you to give you His Peace.

(source unknown)

"...I will never leave you, nor forsake you."
—Hebrews 13:5b

Firmly grasp the hand of Christ
He will not let go.
Hang on to Him.

Lasting Imprints

Ask Yourself…

Have I allowed Jesus to be the shepherd of my life?

Think About It…

Prepare for future storms by allowing God a bigger place in your life.

Remember…

The storm you are facing will be followed by a rainbow. Watch for it.

Respond in Prayer

You are my caring Shepherd,
The Quieter of my storms.
You lead me to green pastures,
And put rainbows in the sky.
…Amen.

Application Questions

Then He arose and rebuked the wind,
and said to the sea, "Peace, be still!"
And the wind ceased and there was a great calm.
—Mark 4:39-40a

1. What are your thoughts about the *Lasting Imprints* on p. 107?

2. Pick a statement in Fingerprint Eight and describe how it applies to your life.

3. What storm is going on in your life right now?

4. How are your storms similar to, or very different from, those of Paul?

5. Describe a time God has calmed storms and given peace to you.

Describe the peace that comes after a storm in your life.

_____

_____

6. Reread the 23rd Psalm and then meditate on it. What new words and concepts do you see that you may not have previously seen in it?

_____

_____

7. Read the benediction on page 105 and then describe each of the positions God takes with you as you go on your path.

_____

_____

_____

8. What fears do you have as you face the life ahead?

_____

_____

Pray that God will give you peace in each of those areas and that you will know Him better through it.

9. What idea from this lesson could you share with a friend?

_____

_____

10. What other action(s) will you take as a result of this lesson?

_____

_____

You gently shaped me
to be teachable.
And fed me from
Your nourishing vine.

He Prunes My Branches

…every branch that bears fruit He prunes…
that it might bear more fruit.
—John 15:2

Gardeners prune plants with the skill of an artisan to remove just the right branches to generate fruitful growth. The skill of the gardener is revealed in how he handles each unique plant with care and insight to remove dead or unproductive branches. The primary benefit of the pruning process in gardening is that it stimulates new growth.

Visitors to the Butchart Gardens in Victoria, British Columbia, have a breath-taking opportunity to experience the work of a master gardener. The vast varieties and colors of flowers create beauty, elegance, and sweet-smelling fragrances throughout the spacious grounds. Guests at the 55-acre botanical masterpiece are greeted by an array of flowers throughout the entire landscape. Beautiful plants adorn the walking paths. Blossoming flowers enhance the natural drama of waterfalls and to add beauty to the plethora of bushes and trees.

Throughout the intricate gardens, trellises support young, tender vines and branches. With meticulous attention the gardeners guide the growth of each vine so that it becomes an integral part of the beautiful landscape. This includes pruning, the careful removal of branches that detract from the overall beauty. This causes the plant to grow stronger and become more fruitful. Each plant grows to maturity according to the master gardener's plan. The beauty that appears to flow naturally throughout the Butchart Gardens, is the result of both an intricate plan and consistent daily care.

Pruning Process

Pruning was a good example for Jesus to use since the people of Israel were familiar with the cultivation of grapes and other produce. Jesus describes His Father as the vinedresser (the good gardener), Himself as the vine, and His followers as the branches. God's tender cutting away of "dead" or "superfluous" parts of your life prepares you to grow and bear spiritual fruit.

God's pruning helps us become more like Jesus in our thoughts and actions. The more we become like Him, the more we are able to serve God. We are able to bear spiritual fruit as the interfering branches are removed. God makes each cut anticipating what the new growth will look like.

God is in the ideal position to recognize the parts of your life that are limiting your potential to serve in His Kingdom. He lovingly prunes you through His Holy Spirit, the Word, pastors and teachers, friends, and circumstances in your life. Through these tools, He helps you recognize and make needed changes.

It was not that I did not know Your ways.

It was not that I did not know Your expectations.

It was that I wanted my own way more than Yours

Now I am yours, want your ways,

and accept your expectations.

Now I am growing and becoming.

Now I am a branch and you are the vine.

I am alive.

Jesus is the Vine

Jesus loves you unconditionally. He will not love you more or less based on what you do. You cannot earn His praise, nor destroy His desire to see you prosper. He wants you to grow in ways which make you a stronger person in Him. He wants to increase your potential to serve Him. It's a sign of true love. We may not even realize the subtle ways God is transforming us. In His wisdom God may use those near us to give us needed help and encouragement to grow.

> Just as the canvas has no fear
> of the artist's brush, so the branch welcomes
> the Gardener's touch.

Jesus is the vine. We receive our spiritual nourishment through Him. By His death and resurrection we have been given the opportunity to be alive spiritually. By trusting in Him we are connected to the Father. Through the Word of God, and the work of the Holy Spirit, we are being fed spiritually. This food helps us grow and prepares us to serve. Just as the vine is a vessel through which food and water can be supplied to nourish the branches, Jesus is the vessel by which God delivers spiritual nourishment to us.

On Lenore's daily morning walk with her dog, Brandy, she noticed a beautiful Morning Glory flower that had fallen on the sidewalk. It added a surprising beauty to the otherwise grayness of the path. Walking on, Lenore thought about that flower. It was no longer attached to its stem and would lose its beauty and fragrance in a just a few hours. We are like that as well. When we are not attached to the True Vine, we will lose the beauty and fragrance of Christ in our life. Like the flower, we are meant to be attached and fed by Him.

Abide in Him

When we allow Jesus to be our source of spiritual nourishment and live according to His commandments, we develop a closer relationship with God. "Abide in Him," means to have a close relationship of "following," "remaining in," and "becoming like," Jesus.

There are several references to "abide" in the Old and New Testaments. In each case it refers to closeness between an individual and God. The person abiding in Christ is so closely aligned with God that there is a "union" with Him. There is unity of purpose, understanding, and action.

To abide in Christ is to cherish
His ways and words, and God Himself.

The Purpose: Bear Fruit

One result of our abiding in Jesus, The Vine, is the influence we will have in the lives of other people. Without Christ as our source of spiritual nourishment, we cannot bear fruit in the lives of others. We cannot give to others that which we have not received ourselves.

By this My Father is glorified,
that you bear much fruit; so you will be My disciples.
—John 15:8

The purpose of pruning by the gardener is to produce a rich harvest of fruit. In the vineyard of the Kingdom, God is the vinedresser. Spiritual fruit is called the "Fruit of the Spirit." These are desirable personal qualities, listed in Galatians 5:22-23, which are developed in followers of Christ as a result of growing in Him.

Pruning Produces Fruit of the Spirit

Love • Joy • Peace

Patience • Kindness

Goodness • Faithfulness

Gentleness • Self-control

As we develop these qualities, we become more fruitful. In the process we become more attractive and pleasant to people around us, including those in our family, at work and school, and others. Therefore, we are better ambassadors for the cause of Christ. We are better able to serve others with His love.

It is the life of the vine flowing through
the branch that produces fruit.
—Millie Stamm

Good fruit is produced by people who live by the truth of God's Word. Bad fruit is produced by those who fail to live by God's truths. (Matthew 7:15-20)

He (who delights in the law of the Lord)
shall be like a tree planted by the rivers of water,
that brings forth its fruit in its season, whose leaf also shall
not wither; and whatever he does shall prosper.
—Psalm 1:3

Conditions for Growth

God will bring about growth if we submit ourselves to His Word and to His instructions. God does not create these difficult situations to teach us a lesson nor to punish us. Rather, when difficult circumstances arise, God is there to help us deal with and to learn from the situation.

> **Growth Situations**
> Challenges and Defeat…Poor Health and Illness…
> Death of Loved Ones…Family Problems…
> Difficult People and Misunderstandings…
> Financial Challenges…God's "No" to Prayer Requests

Trust in God…Believe in Jesus…Live in faith.

God may use the most challenging and difficult experiences to bring about growth and preparation. Bill Bright wrote about this:

Our disappointments are often God's appointments. He is far more concerned about the quality of our eternal future than He is about our present comfort. In fact, difficulties and suffering are tools with which He shapes us into the image of Jesus Christ… Adversity is the touchstone of character.

> As the vine is available to the branch,
> so Christ is available to the one praying.

God does not require that we are spiritually mature to serve Him. Rather, He desires that we grow in understanding and wisdom. We are able to serve Him and others as we are shaped by His pruning shears and fed by His Word.

"What fruit do you see in your life? Do you see how God may be pruning you so that you can bear more and better fruit? Grow closer to Jesus. Yield your life to Him, and allow Him to do anything in your life if it will lead to bearing more fruit."

—Max Lucado

Lasting Imprints

Ask Yourself…

>   Am I becoming the person God intended?

Think About It…

>   With loving hands, God is shaping you.

Remember…

>   When you are attached to the vine of Christ,
>   you glorify God with your fruit.

Respond in Prayer

>   *You are the Gardener of my heart.*
>   *You whisper Your will into my ear.*
>   *The fruit I bear is planned by You,*
>   *grown with Your tender loving care.*
>   *…Amen.*

Fingerprint Nine
Application Questions

Every branch in Me that does not bear fruit He takes away;
and every branch that bears fruit He prunes,
that it may bear more fruit.
—John 15:2

1. What are your thoughts about the *Lasting Imprints* on p. 121?

2. Pick a statement in Fingerprint Nine and describe how it applies to your life.

3. What is meant by the phrase "He prunes my branches?"

4. Do you recognize "branches" that have been pruned, are being pruned, or should be pruned in your life?

5. What does John 15:1-2 mean to you? What does it mean to "abide in Him?" What Bible passages support your view?

6. Name the "fruit of the spirit" found in Galatians 5:22-23.

7. What are you doing to produce good "growth conditions" in your life? What could you do better?

8. What are the sources of "nutrition" for growth that are present or missing at this current time in your life? Consider the quote from Max Lucado on p. 120.

9. What idea from this lesson could you share with a friend?

10. What other action(s) will you take as a result of this lesson?

HE USES ME
Evidence of His Love

*I*n the first section, "He Shows Me," we explored five fingerprints as evidence that God is present. These fingerprints show us there really is a God who cares. In the second section, "He Prepares Me," we described four ways God works to change you into His image. Changes are part of His handiwork as He prepares you to serve His kingdom. In this third section, we learn how "He Uses Me." When you are available to serve Him, God uses you to leave His fingerprints on the people around you.

You taught me
to serve with gladness,

And to leave Your
fingerprints of love.

Serve with Gladness...
Leave His Fingerprints

Serve the Lord with gladness...
—Psalm 100:2

The artist's first lines and paint strokes tell you very little about what he or she has in mind. The artist adds a touch or makes a correction with a brush or finger. Only the artist can make these improvements and add the final touches. The full impact is only revealed when the work of art is complete.

Think of yourself as God's canvas. You are His creation and He has been at work changing you as He prepares you for service. By the brush strokes of Jesus in your life, your purpose is to become all He intended. God's touch on your life is very personal. As you are attentive to Him, He reveals the picture of what He wants you to become. As you abide in Him you become one of His true masterpieces.

For we are God's masterpiece,
He has created us anew in Christ Jesus,
So we can do the good things He planned for us long ago.
—Ephesians 2:10 NLT

Whom Will You Serve?

In the Old Testament Joshua reminded the children of Israel of God's history of faithfulness to them. Joshua exhorted them to follow His example:

...choose for yourselves this day whom you will serve...
But as for me and my house, we will serve the Lord.
—Joshua 24:15 a, d

It is a choice and a commitment God asks from you each day. There are many alternatives. We might choose to serve some other god or human being, work, or money. Serving God means making Him your first priority. That choice influences everything else in your life, including money, friends, values, and entertainment.

Be intentional. Continuously evaluate the way you are using your time and money. Let renewal be the norm. Then daily choices will fall into place. We actually serve Christ when we serve others. It is an act of love born of your relationship with Christ.

Jesus Served with Humility

Serving with humility is a demonstration of love. It is placing another's needs above our own. In so doing, we submit to the will of the One who sacrificed for all. Jesus modeled service many times and in many ways, but His greatest act of service was the sacrifice of His own life. The Bible says there is no greater love than a man laying down his life for another. Even though Jesus was without sin, He gave his life for the sins of all who would receive Him. (John 3:16)

Just prior to His death, Jesus and His disciples celebrated the Jewish Passover. The mood was solemn with the remembrance of God saving the firstborn Jewish sons in Egypt. Then the atmosphere turned even more somber when Jesus said one of the disciples would betray Him. "...Jesus knew that His hour had come and that He would leave this world to return to His Father...He poured water into a basin and began to wash His disciples' feet." (John 13:1, 5) He softly whispered "I did not come to be served, but to serve." (Matthew 20:28, paraphrased) Washing their feet was a tremendous act of service.

> Jesus left the fingerprints of God.
> Those who love Him will do the same.

Even today it is noticeable when modern-day leaders serve with humility. Campus Crusade for Christ president, Steve Douglas, wrote about one of the many times the organization's founder, Bill Bright, modeled humility. On their first trip together to Japan, they were joined by two other staff members. Bill retired first to the sleeping area. When the others retired for the night, they found Bill had taken the worst bed, a top bunk. While his position warranted the best bed, a floor-level, queen-sized bed, he had chosen the inconvenient and smaller bed. Bill had shown in this small example that he lived by Paul's exhortation, "In humility consider others better than yourselves." (Philippians 2:3)

I will bless you ... and you will be a blessing to others.
—Genesis 12:2 NLT

Equipped for Service

We need to be clear about the ways God can use us to serve Him. He wants a committed and willing heart. When we have a willing heart, He will use us in a variety of ways.

When you offer your gifts and talents to God, He gives you ways to serve.

One day after her morning devotions, Lenore was looking at her calendar. God impressed upon her heart to go visit her 90-year-old friend. She admits she argued a little with God and explained to Him that "I was just there the day before" (as though He didn't know that fact). But the feeling persisted; "Go visit Rose!" Finally choosing to follow the nudge, she got in the car and went to see Rose. As she walked in, Rose said "I've been praying all day that someone would come. My glasses are downtown and I have no one to go get them for me."

Divine appointments are those times when God asks you to serve Him by serving others. They are the times when He asks you to use your talents and gifts to bless someone else. We all have doctor's appointments, meetings to attend, and errands to run. What if God adds something to your schedule? Are you willing to say "Here I am, send me?"

Another way we serve God is with our worship. We can worship Him privately or with others. It may include prayer, music, scripture, and even dancing. In fact, worship encompasses all forms of communication with God. Even the way we live our life can be a form of worship.

> **Music** is the universal language
> of the heart.
>
> **Dance** is the universal language
> of the body.
>
> **Prayer** is the universal language
> of the spirit.

We are not alone as we go about serving the Lord. Mark 16:20 (NLT) states, "And the disciples went everywhere and preached, and the Lord worked through them…" The Lord can also work through us as we encounter opportunities to serve Him and people He places in our lives.

There are as many unique ways to serve God as there are individuals in the Kingdom. In addition to talents at birth, and the ones developed over a lifetime, God has gifted each believer with special gifts of service. They are given to both glorify God and be a blessing to others. These gifts are not for your benefit, but for building the body of Christ. They are bestowed on believers by the Holy Spirit. (Romans 12:6-8, 1 Corinthians 12:8-10 28, and Ephesians 4:11-12) No person or gift is more important than another. All are needed for the Body to function effectively.

You should not attempt to do someone else's role, but to be gracious in doing that to which you have been called. You will be most effective when you are guided by the Holy Spirit to utilize your unique gifts. That means some will teach Sunday school, play the organ, serve on committees and boards, pray for needs, or reach out with a kind word to a hurting soul. But everyone will have opportunities to serve the Lord as we meet the needs of the people in our midst. The important part is to obey your calling to serve.

Ready to Serve: Availability

God can use your gifts and talents, but only when you are available to serve Him.

You never know precisely when you are going to be used by God. That is why you need to be available to serve. It may not be the next thing on your list, and it may not be what you had hoped He would ask of you.

God knows your talents and is looking for your *availability*. He wants people who will interrupt their busy day to give their attention and commitment to Him. God will equip you with just what you need.

> *Availability* is your most
> important act of service.

Lenore took a demonstration ride with a car salesman who seemed very sad and troubled. Lenore felt compelled to tell him about Jesus, but gave herself excuses like "I do not have my Bible. I am not prepared." Finally, she began sharing her faith through what felt like stumbling words. The salesman listened with tears in his eyes to the hope offered by Christ. God can use you even when you don't feel adequate or prepared!

> God's timing is always perfect.

Supporting Others

Regardless of your role, God has set you apart for service. At times you may be "center stage" for the Lord. When this occurs, remember all the accolades belong to Him. Other times you may merely be part of the "supporting cast." Your talents, gifts, and opportunities to serve will most likely include some unnoticed activities. But don't be mistaken. God views your unique place in the big picture as important.

One of the examples of a supporting role occurred in Exodus 17 when Moses told Joshua to pick some men to go into battle against the Amalekites. Moses explained that, "Tomorrow I will stand on the top of the hill with the rod of God in my hand." (Exodus 17:9b) The next morning Moses, Aaron, and Hur climbed to the top of the hill. Moses did just as he said, but he became tired and could no longer hold up his hands. Every time his hands started coming down, the army of Israel started losing the battle. Only when Aaron and Hur stood beside Moses and supported his arms, and the upraised rod of God, was their army successful.

Holding up Moses' arms may not seem very important, but it was the difference between success and failure. Many important parts are "back stage" or seemingly insignificant. Our calling will most likely include some of these unnoticed activities. Where is it that you need to be in a supporting role? Perhaps there is someone who is so tired or weak, and they need "their hands held up." Do your part so that God's purposes might be achieved.

> *...for I was hungry and you gave Me food;*
> *I was thirsty and gave Me drink;*
> *I was a stranger and You took Me in...*
> *—Matthew 25:35*

Remember, even when you give someone a drink of water in His name, you are serving the Lord. Who is God telling you to encourage? Who does He want you to support in their role?

When you leave God's fingerprints,
it is evidence of His love within you,
revealed to those you touch for Him.

They are Fingerprints of Faith.

Lasting Imprints

Ask Yourself…

Am I on my knees preparing for service?

Think About It…

The greatest honor to the Lord is to use the gifts He has given you.

Remember…

You are His masterpiece.

Respond in Prayer

My heart is filled with gladness because
You gave purpose to my life.
May I serve You by touching lives,
Leaving Your fingerprints of faith.
…Amen.

Fingerprint Ten
Application Questions

Serve the Lord with gladness;
Come before His presence with singing.
—Psalm 100:2

1. What are your thoughts about the *Lasting Imprints* on p. 137?

    _____

    _____

    _____

2. Pick a statement in Fingerprint Ten and describe how it applies to your life.

    _____

    _____

    _____

3. Why do you think we should serve with joy and gladness?

    _____

    _____

4. How do we "leave His fingerprints" when we serve others?

    _____

    _____

5. What does Ephesians 4:1 mean to you? What is a "worthy calling" for you?

    _____

    _____

    _____

6. In what ways do you see yourself uniquely equipped and capable of serving?

    In what ways do you see yourself "supporting" others in their service?

7. How do you demonstrate your "availability" to serve others and to serve the Lord?

    Are there ways you can be more available?

8. How does your worship reflect serving the Lord with joy?

9. What idea from this lesson could you share with a friend?

10. What other action(s) will you take as a result of this lesson?

I take joy in doing Your will, my God;
Your fingerprints are written on my heart
as evidence of your love.
—Psalm 40:8, paraphrased

Fingerprints of Faith Prayer

By Lenore Else

O Lord, You spoke the majesty of Your creation,
    Galaxies, land, and seas sprang forth.
You fashioned me before I was born,
    And placed eternity upon my heart.
You gave me Your Word as a guide.
    It brings light to my daily life.
You want me to abide in Your love.
    And in profound love, died in my place.
You said, "Come, walk, talk with Me.
    Tell Me the questions of your heart."
You saw past all my stubborn ways,
    And gave me a tender, responsive heart.
You said to trust You with all my heart.
    I said "Yes Lord, make Your ways known."
You held my hand during the storms,
    Leading me to still and quiet waters.
You gently shaped me to be teachable.
    And fed me from Your nourishing vine.
You taught me to serve with gladness…
    And to leave Your fingerprints of love. **Amen.**

References

Bright, Bill, *God: Discover His Character*, New Life Publications, Orlando, FL, 1999, ISBN 1-56399-121-7, p. 117.

Chow, David, Executive Director of Ambassadors for Christ, Ambassadors For Christ Prayer Calendar email on Friday, May 1, 2009.

Douglas, Steve, President of Campus Crusade for Christ, *Connections*, Campus Crusade for Christ, April 2009, Vol. 9, No. 4.

Gerbens, Larry, *The Father & His Two Sons: The Art of Forgiveness*, Eyekons Publishing, Grand Rapids, Michigan, 2009, ISBN 978-1-60725-565-9.

Graham, Billy, *Decision Magazine*, 2001 and Hope for the Troubled Heart, Word Publishing, Nashville, TN, 1991, ISBN – 0-553-56155-3.

Lewis, C. S. Author of *Mere Christianity*. The original source of this quote is not known. Found in www.famousquotesandauthors.com, C.S. Lewis quotes.

Lucado, Max, General Editor, *The Devotional Bible*, *Experiencing the Heart of Jesus*, New Century Version, Thomas Nelson Bibles, Nashville, TN, 2003, ISBN 0-7180-0961-4.

Newberry, Tommy, *The 4:8 Principle: The Secret to a Joy-Filled* Life, Tyndale House Publishers, Inc., Carol Stream, IL, 2007, ISBN 978-1-4143-1304-7, p. 24.

Henri Nouwen, *The Return of the Prodigal: A Story of Homecoming*, Doubleday, New York, 1992, p. 16, ISBN – 0-385-47307-9.

Spurgeon, Charles, Original source is not known, This concept is also presented in a sermon by Everett L. Fullam, "Come! See! Go! Tell!" Preaching Tape #19, Matthew 28:1-7.

Stamm, Millie, *Be Still and Know*, Zondervan Publishing House, Grand Rapids, Michigan, 1978, Entry for August 27. ISBN Cloth – 0-310-32990-6, Paper – 0-310-32991-4.

Stovall, Jim, *The Ultimate Gift*, David C. Cook, Colorado Springs, CO, 2001, ISBN – 978-0-7814-4563-4937539484.

Tada, Joni Erickson, *Pearls of Great Price*, Zondervan, Grand Rapids, MI, 2006, July 16, ISBN 978-0-310-26298-5.

About the Authors

Jim Sheard holds a doctorate degree in industrial psychology. Over the course of a 30-year career, he was a university associate professor, human resources consultant to organizations, and corporate executive, most recently President of Federated Insurance Companies. He retired from business in 1996 and began writing and speaking. Jim is the co-author of five highly-acclaimed gift books published by Word Publishing, J. Countryman. They are *In His Grip*, *Playing the Game*, *A Champion's Heart*, *Finishing the Course*, and *The Master's Grip*. Jim is also the co-author of the golf portions of *The Golfer's Bible* which is a complete Old and New Testament published as one of B-H Publisher's theme Bibles.

Jim's favorite Bible verse:
Be strong and of good courage...
the Lord your God is with you wherever you go.
—Joshua 1:9 RSV

Lenore Else is an accomplished writer and business owner with a degree in speech therapy. She is the Chairman and co-founder of EI Microcircuits in Mankato and in St. Peter, MN. Lenore has developed numerous Bible studies, prayers, and articles. She is currently completing a compendium of daily prayers for her grandchildren, *To All Generations*. Lenore was a lecturer for the "Search Bible Studies" and taught many Bible studies, including the "Bethel Bible Study" series. She is an online counselor for Campus Crusade and has traveled the world with Campus Crusade for Christ and International Cooperating Ministries (ICM). The Jesus Film Project awarded Lenore and her late husband "The Hope Medallion" for their service to help bring hope to the world through Jesus Christ.

Lenore's favorite Bible verse:
Trust in the Lord with all your heart,
and do not lean on your own understanding.
—*Proverbs 3:5 ESV*

Submit Your
Fingerprints of Faith Story

We encourage you to write a story of how you have experienced *Fingerprints of Faith* in your life. A fingerprint of faith story may tell an experience of God actively working in your life. It may be a story of how "He Shows Me," "He Prepares Me," or "He Uses Me." Your story might explain *The Evidence of Things Not Seen* as it is occurring in your life.

Submit your story (200 words or less) on our web site, www.fingerprintsoffaith.org. We retain the right to edit your story for length or other reasons and may use it on our website or in a future publication. You must provide your name and email address, but they will not be shown in any printing of the story.

Others will be encouraged by your testimony of how God has been at work in your life!

My Reflections

_____

_____

_____

_____

_____

_____

_____

_____

_____

_____

_____

_____

_____

_____

_____

_____

_____

_____

_____